The Dedalus Press

Lorca: The Tamarit Poems

translated from Spanish by Michael Smith

Poetry Europe 11

The Tamarit Poems

by
Federico García Lorca

translated by
Michael Smith

A version of Diván del Tamarit

With an Afterword
by
Emilio García Gómez

The Dedalus Press
24 The Heath, Cypress Downs, Dublin 6W
Ireland

ISBN 1 901233 86 3

COVER DRAWING BY TONY O'MALLEY

Dedalus Press books are distributed in the U.K. by
Central Books, Ltd. 99 Wallis Road, London E9 5LN,
and in the U.S.A. and Canada by
Dufour Editions Inc., PO Box 7, Chester Springs,
Pennsylvania 19425 – 0007

The Dedalus Press receives financial assistance from An
Chomhairle Ealaíon, The Arts Council, Ireland

Printed by The Johnswood Press, Dublin

for Alice
as a reminder of our summers in Andalusia

ACKNOWLEDGEMENTS:

The Spanish text is that of Miguel García-Posada, *Obras II*, Madrid, 1982.

Without burdening him with any responsibility for my errors, I wish to thank my good friend Luis Huerga who once again, with incalculable generosity of goodwill, time, energy, patience and skill, has been my guide through another Spanish literary labyrinth.

The Irish poet Trevor Joyce initiated the present translation by communicating to me his enthusiasm for this too-little known poetry of Lorca, which may very well turn out to be the Granadine poet's masterpiece.

I also wish to express my thanks Don José Paulino of the *Universidad Complutense* of Madrid who was kind enough to fill in many a blank in my information.

Finally, I wish to express my gratitude towards the late Don Emilio García Gómez. In particular I wish to acknowledge his kind permission to print my translation of his fine essay on the Tamarit poems, and for his generous response to the idea of bringing out, though not for the first time I must admit, these poems in a single volume as originally intended by all concerned. I consider this present book as a form of *homenaje* to a great Spanish scholar and translator.

CONTENTS

PREFACE

Lorca, notwithstanding the vigorous persuasion of Roy Campbell and others, was never a simple folk, much less a simple local poet who got lost for a time in the big complex outside world of avant-garde experimentation as demonstrated, it is alleged, by *Poet in New York*. On the contrary, from the beginning, Lorca was a conscious literary craftsman who delighted in experimentation. His *Gypsy Ballads*, however it struck and still strikes many readers, is not simple folk stuff, but work that is as elaborately wrought as the *romances* or ballads of that consummate master of the baroque, Luis de Góngora, Lorca's favourite poet of the *siglo de oro*. It is of course true that in the Tamarit poems Lorca manifestly returns to Andalusian material, specifically to his native city of Granada, for images and atmosphere, among other things; and it is also true that traditional ballad rhythms can once more be heard in the *gacelas* and *casidas*; yet it is equally true to say that the Lorca of the *Poeta en Nueva York* is very definitely present in this posthumously published Granadine book of his in which experimentation in rhythm and images and other techniques is just as evident, if more self-assuredly controlled than in the New York poems.

In Lorca's Tamarit poems, the broad and dominant theme is that of life/love and death. These polarities are clearly in evidence throughout the poems: night and day, earth and moon, light and dark, warmth and cold, morning and evening, laughter and tears, opening and closing. The images that proliferate are those of elemental air, fire, water* and earth.

---

* Images of water are inseparable from Granada: water in irrigation channels, in pools, in streams; this has been so from the time of the Romans and the Moors and throughout its Christian history.

Speaking of Góngora, Lorca says *Todas las imágenes se abren, pues, en el campo visual* ('All images unfold in the visual field'). It is the transmutability of the images in Lorca that exercises such a powerful fascination for readers. They do not, however, transfer into statements; they resist logical sequentiality and causality: they are not, in short, paraphrasable in other terms. That said, a tentative thematic framework of sorts may be helpful so long as it is not misused to reduce the poems in any way.

The passion of a love tormented seems to underpin most of the poems in the Tamarit collection, as indeed it does most of Lorca's work. The nature of that love is never unequivocally stated, and the reader would be well advised to keep an open mind on this. It seems to me to be enough to know that it is love unfulfilled. Unsatisfied desire is experienced as a kind of death. But while the tone of Lorca's poems is strongly elegiac, it is never melancholic: the poems are always astir with imagistic defiance:

Blood will ring in the alcoves
and appear with lightning sword.

(Casida IV)

The 'dark child' of Gacela VIII, the 'new-born child' of Gacela X, the 'wounded child' of Casida I, the 'children with veiled faces' of Casida III and the 'young girl' of Casidas V, VIII and IX: these allusions point to a longing to escape from the problematic consciousness of the adult, back to the prelapsarian world of childhood in which the child can lose himself or herself in the world of nature. For Lorca, as for Dylan

10

Thomas, the innocence of childhood — in the etymological sense of a state of 'unhurt' — always exercised tremendous attraction. One's instincts, then, may be guiltlessly vital, unfettered; the world for the child may be vibrantly alive and magical, as in Dylan Thomas's magnificent 'Fern Hill'.

These generalities, which are intended as no more than a rough introductory thematic framework, will have to suffice in a brief Preface such as this. What is perhaps more interesting, though this, too, must be left to the reader to explore further, is how the poems render change without recourse to narrative, and how, also, they manage to convey many complex ideas without recourse to abstract language. The key to both, I think, lies in repetition, parallelism and alternation. The repetition functions within a given poem, and between poems. With parallelism, a structure is set up which is repeated, but with significant differences. These differences can, amongst other things, locate a different point in a process (passage of time, perhaps). Alternation works through the use of two distinct structures which interface with one another throughout the poems, sometimes achieving a final resolution through some combination of the two (Gacela III).

Lorca's conscious employment of these techniques derives largely from Spanish *romances* and other folkloric sources, as well as from Lorca's reading of Bécquer and his study of Góngora. The undeniable influence of surrealism on Lorca, unlike its influence on his friends and contemporaries, Dalí and Buñuel, was not systematically assimilated or applied, but rather gave him a sense of freedom to experiment further, to go beyond the *gitanismo* with which he felt himself burdened as a poet.

11

Finally, with Lorca's Tamarit poems in front of me, it seems to me very apposite to quote Wittgenstein's remark about the equally enigmatic poems of the Austrian Georg Trakl: "I do not understand them," Wittgenstein said, "but their tone delights me. It is the tone of a man of real genius."

Michael Smith

Dublin

I GACELA DEL AMOR IMPREVISTO

Nadie comprendía el perfume
de la oscura magnolia de tu vientre.
Nadie sabía que martirizabas
un colibrí de amor entre los dientes.

Mil caballitos persas se dormían
en la plaza con luna de tu frente
mientras que yo enlazaba cuatro noches
tu cintura enemiga de la nieve.

Entre yeso y jazmines, tu mirada
era en pálido ramo de simientes.
Yo busqué para darte por mi pecho
las letras de marfil que dicen *siempre,*

siempre, siempre, jardín de mi agonía,
tu cuerpo fugitivo para siempre,
la sangre de tus venas en mi boca,
tu boca ya sin luz para mi muerte.

I   *GACELA OF LOVE UNFORESEEN*

No one understood the fragrance
of your belly's dark magnolia.
No one knew you were torturing
a hummingbird of love between your teeth.

A thousand Persian ponies were dozing
in the moonlit square of your brow,
while for four nights I was embracing
your waist, enemy of snow.

Your gaze, between plaster and jasmine,
was a pale cluster of seeds.
On my chest I sought to give you
letters of ivory saying 'forever.

Forever, forever': garden of my anguish,
your fleeting body forever,
the blood of your veins in my mouth,
your mouth without light to my death.

II   GACELA DE LA TERRIBLE PRESENCIA

Yo quiero que el agua se quede sin cauce.
Yo quiero que el viento se quede sin valles.

Quiero que la noche se quede sin ojos
y mi corazón sin la flor del oro.

Que los bueyes hablen con las grandes hojas
y que la lombriz se muera de sombra.

Que brillen los dientes de la calavera
y los amarillos inunden la seda.

Puedo ver el duelo de la noche herida
luchando enroscada con el mediodía.

Resisto un ocaso de verde veneno
y los arcos rotos donde sufre el tiempo.

Pero no me enseñes tu limpio desnudo
como un negro cactus abierto en los juncos.

Déjame en un ansia de oscuros planetas,
¡pero no me enseñes tu cintura fresca!

II   GACELA OF THE TERRIBLE PRESENCE

I want the stream to lose its banks.
I want no slopes to cradle the wind.

I would have the night eyeless
and my heart yield up its fine gold;

oxen converse with broad leaves
and the worm die of shadow;

the skull's teeth glitter
and the yellows flood the silk.

I can bear to see the grief of wounded night
struggling in the coils of noon.

I withstand a sunset of green venom
and shattered arches where Time mourns.

But do not show me your lucent nakedness
as a black cactus opened out in rushes.

Leave me to yearn for dark planets
but do not show me your young waist!

III *GACELA DEL AMOR DESESPERADO*

La noche no quiere venir
para que tú no vengas
ni yo pueda ir.

Pero yo iré
aunque un sol de alacranes me coma la sien.
Pero tú vendrás
con la lengua quemada por la lluvia de sal.

El día no quiere venir
para que tú no vengas
ni yo pueda ir.

Pero yo iré
entregando a los sapos mi mordido clavel.
Pero tú vendrás
por las turbias cloacas de la oscuridad.

Ni la noche ni el día quieren venir
para que por ti muera
y tú mueras por mí.

III *GACELA OF DESPERATE LOVE*

Night doesn't want to come
that you may not come
that I may not go.

But I will go,
though a scorpion sun bites my temples.
But you shall come,
with your tongue burnt by salt rain.

Day doesn't want to come
that you may not come
that I may not go.

But I will go,
yielding to toads my chewed carnation.
But you shall come
through the murky sewers of darkness.

Neither night nor day wants to come
that I may die for you
and you may die for me.

IV   *GACELA DEL AMOR QUE NO SE DEJA VER*

Solamente por oír
la campana de la Vela
te puse una corona de verbena.

Granada era una luna
ahogada entre las yedras.

Solamente por oír
la campana de la Vela
desgarré mi jardín de Cartagena.

Granada era una corza
rosa por las veletas.

Solamente por oír
la campana de la Vela
me abrasaba en tu cuerpo
sin saber de quién era.

IV *GACELA OF THE LOVE THAT WILL NOT BE EXPOSED*

Only to hear
the bell of the Vela
I placed on your head a crown of verbena.

Granada was a moon
choking in the ivy.

Only to hear
the bell of the Vela
I tore open my garden of Cartagena.

Granada was a hind
pink over the weathervanes.

Only to hear
the bell of the Vela
I burned in your flesh
not knowing it was yours.

V GACELA DEL NIÑO MUERTO

Todas las tardes en Granada,
todas las tardes se muere un niño.
Todas las tardes el agua se sienta
a conversar con sus amigos.

Los muertos llevan dos alas de musgo.
El viento nublado y el viento limpio
son dos faisanes que vuelan por las torres
y el día es un muchacho herido.

No quedaba en el aire ni una brizna de alondra
cuando yo te encontré por las grutas del vino.
No quedaba en la tierra ni una miga de nube
cuando te ahogabas por el río.

Un gigante de agua cayó sobre los montes
y el valle fue rodando con perros y con lirios.
Tu cuerpo, con la sombra violeta de mis manos,
era, muerto en la orilla, un arcángel de frío.

V GACELA OF THE DEAD CHILD

Every afternoon in Granada,
every afternoon a child dies.
Every afternoon the water sits
to speak with its friends.

The dead wear wings of moss.
The cloudy wind and the clear wind
are two pheasants that fly through the towers
and day is a wounded boy.

There was not a shred of lark in the air
when I found you in the wine caverns.
There was not a crumb of cloud on the land
when you drowned in the river.

A water-giant fell on the mountains
and the valley rolled away with dogs and lilies.
Your body, with the dark violet of my hands,
was, dead on the bank, an archangel of cold.

VI   *GACELA DE LA RAÍZ AMARGA*

Hay una raíz amarga
y un mundo de mil terrazas.

Ni la mano más pequeña
quiebra la puerta del agua.

¿Dónde vas? ¿adónde? ¿dónde?
Hay un cielo de mil ventanas
— batalla de abejas lívidas —
y hay una raíz amarga.

Amarga.

Duele en la planta del pie,
el interior de la cara
y duele en el tronco fresco
de noche recién cortada.

¡Amor! Enemigo mío
¡muerde tu raíz amarga!

VI *GACELA OF THE BITTER ROOT*

There is a bitter root
and a thousand-terraced world.

Even the smallest hand
cannot cleave the barring water.

Where are you going, where, where?
There is a thousand-windowed sky
— livid bees in combat —
and there is a bitter root.

Bitter.

On the sole of the foot
the inner face pains,
and there's pain in the living trunk
as of night just felled.

Love, enemy of mine,
chew on your bitter root.

VII   *GACELA DEL RECUERDO DE AMOR*

No te lleves tu recuerdo.
Déjalo solo en mi pecho.

Temblor de blanco cerezo
en el martirio de Enero.

Me separa de los muertos
un muro de malos sueños.

Doy pena de lirio fresco
para un corazón de yeso.

Toda la noche en el huerto
mis ojos como dos perros.

Toda la noche comiendo
los membrillos de veneno.

Algunas veces el viento
es un tulipán de miedo.
Es un tulipán enfermo
la madrugada de invierno.

Un muro de malos sueños
me separa de los muertos.

VII   *GACELA OF LOVE'S MEMORY*

Don't take away your memory.
Leave it alone in my chest.

A tremor of white cherry
in punishing January.

A wall of evil dreams
cuts me off from the dead.

My fresh-lily sorrow
is for plaster hearts.

All night in the orchard
my eyes, like two dogs.

All night, eating
the quince of poison.

Sometimes the wind
is a tulip of fear.

It is a sick tulip,
the early morning of winter.

A wall of evil dreams
cuts me off from the dead.

La hierba cubre en silencio
el valle gris de tu cuerpo.

Por el arco del encuentro
la cicuta está creciendo.

Pero deja tu recuerdo.
¡Déjalo solo en mi pecho!

Grass covers in silence
the grey valley of your body.

Along the meeting arch
the hemlock is growing.

But leave your memory,
leave it alone in my chest.

VIII _GACELA DE LA MUERTE OSCURA_

Quiero dormir el sueño de las manzanas,
alejarme del tumulto de los cementerios.
Quiero dormir el sueño de aquel niño
que quería cortarse el corazón en alta mar.

No quiero que me repitan que los muertos no pierden la san-
gre,
que la boca podrida sigue pidiendo agua.
No quiero enterarme de los martirios que da la hierba
ni de la luna con boca de serpiente
que trabaja antes del amanecer.

Quiero dormir un rato,
un rato, un minuto, un siglo,
pero que todos sepan que no he muerto
que hay un establo de oro en mis labios
que soy el pequeño amigo del viento Oeste
que soy la sombra inmensa de mis lágrimas.

Cúbreme por la aurora con un velo
porque me arrojará puñados de hormigas
y moja con agua dura mis zapatos
para que resbale la pinza de su alacrán.

Porque quiero dormir el sueño de las manzanas
para aprender un llanto que me limpie de tierra,
porque quiero vivir con aquel niño oscuro
que quería cortarse el corazón en alta mar.

VIII *GACELA OF DARK DEATH*

I long to sleep the sleep of apples,
go far away from the turmoil of cemeteries.
I long to sleep the sleep of that child
who longed to cut his heart on the high sea.

I do not want to hear that the dead lose no blood,
that the putrid mouth goes on thirsting.
I do not want to know of torments grass produces,
nor of the moon with its serpent mouth
at work before dawn.

I long to sleep a little while,
a little while, a minute, a century,
yet all should know I have not died;
know there's a golden stable on my lips,
that I'm the West Wind's little friend,
the vast shadow of my tears.

Cover me with a veil at dawn,
for it will fling at me fistfuls of ants,
and wet my shoes with hard water
so that its scorpion's pincer may slip.

Because I long to sleep the sleep of apples
to learn a flood of tears cleansing me of earth;
because I long to live with that dark child
who longed to cut his heart on the high sea.

IX   *GACELA DEL AMOR MARAVILLOSO*

Con todo el yeso
de los malos campos
eras junco de amor, jazmín mojado.

Con sur y llama
de los malos cielos
eras rumor de nieve por mi pecho.

Cielos y campos
anudaban cadenas en mis manos.

Campos y cielos
azotaban las llagas de mi cuerpo.

IX *G*ACELA *OF* M*ARVELLOUS* L*OVE*

With all the clay
of the bad fields,
you were a reed of love, a moist jasmine.

With south and blaze
of the bad skies,
you were a murmur of snow about my chest.

Skies and fields
bound chains on my hands.

Fields and skies
lashed the sores of my body.

X   *GACELA DE LA HUIDA*

Me he perdido muchas veces por el mar
con el oído lleno de flores recién cortadas.
Con la lengua llena de amor y de agonía
muchas veces me he perdido por el mar,
como me pierdo en el corazón de algunos niños.

No hay nadie que al dar un beso
no sienta la sonrisa de la gente sin rostro,
ni hay nadie que al tocar un recién nacido
olvide las inmóviles calaveras de caballo.

Porque las rosas buscan en la frente
un duro paisaje de hueso
y las manos del hombre no tienen más sentido
que imitar a las raíces bajo tierra.

Como me pierdo en el corazón de algunos niños,
me he perdido muchas veces por el mar.
Ignorante del agua, voy buscando
una muerte de luz que me consuma.

X   *GACELA OF THE FLIGHT*

I have often lost myself in the sea
with my ears full of fresh-cut flowers.
My tongue full of love and anguish,
often I have lost myself in the sea
as I lose myself in some children's heart.

No night, when giving a kiss,
do I not feel the smile of the faceless;
nor, on touching the new-born child,
can one forget the motionless skulls of horses.

Because the roses trace on the brow
a hard landscape of bone
and our hands can do no more
than mime the roots beneath the earth.

As I lose myself in some children's heart,
I have often lost myself in the sea.
Oblivious of the water, I am seeking
a death of light to consume me.

XI GACELA DEL AMOR CON CIEN AÑOS

Suben por la calle
los cautro galanes,

ay, ay, ay, ay.

Por la calle abajo
van los tres galanes,

ay, ay, ay.

Se ciñen el talle
esos dos galanes,

ay, ay.

¡Cómo vuelve el rostro
un galán y el aire!

ay.

En los arrayanes
se pasea nadie.

XI *Gacela of a Hundred-Year Love*

Up the street
stride the four young bucks,

ay, ay, ay, ay.

Down the street
stroll the three young bucks,

ay, ay, ay.

They entwine their waists,
those two young bucks,

ay, ay.

How he swivels his head,
one young buck, and his poise!

ay.

Through the myrtles
strolls no one.

XII *GACELA DEL MERCADO MATUTINO*

Por el arco de Elvira
quiero verte pasar
para saber tu nombre
y ponerme a llorar.

¿Qué luna gris de las nueve
te desangró la mejilla?
¿Quién recoge tu semilla
de llamarada en la nieve?
¿Qué alfiler de cactus breve
asesina tu cristal?

Por el arco de Elvira
voy a verte pasar
para beber tus ojos
y ponerme a llorar.

¡Qué voz para mi castigo
levantas por el mercado!
¡Qué clavel enajenado
en los montones de trigo!
¡Qué lejos estoy contigo!
¡qué cerca cuando te vas!

Por el arco de Elvira
voy a verte pasar
para sufrir tus muslos
y ponerme a llorar.

XII *GACELA OF THE MORNING MARKET*

Under the Elvira arch
let me see you pass
that I may learn your name
and cry.

What pale moon at nine
bled your cheek white?
Who gathers up the seed
that sets its snow aflame?
What tiny cactus spike
shatters your glass?

Under the Elvira arch
let me see you pass
that I may lap your eyes
and cry.

How it chastens me,
the market-call you raise!
What odd carnation, you,
amid the piles of wheat!
How far you are when close!
How near to me when gone!

Under the Elvira arch
let me see you pass
that I may suffer your thighs
and cry.

I CASIDA DEL HERIDO POR EL AGUA

Quiero bajar al pozo
quiero subir los muros de Granada
para mirar el corazón pasado
por el punzón oscuro de las aguas.

El niño herido gemía
con una corona de escarcha.
Estanques, aljibes y fuentes
levantaban al aire sus espadas.
¡Ay qué furia de amor! ¡qué hiriente filo!
¡qué nocturno rumor! ¡qué muerte blanca!
¡qué desiertos de luz iban hundiendo
los arenales de la madrugada!
El niño estaba solo
con la ciudad dormida en la garganta.
Un surtidor que viene de los sueños
lo defiende del hambre de las algas.
El niño y su agonía frente a frente
eran dos verdes lluvias enlazadas.
El niño se tendía por la tierra
y su agonía se curvaba.

Quiero bajar al pozo
quiero morir mi muerte a bocanadas
quiero llenar mi corazón de musgo
para ver al herido por el agua.

I *CASIDA OF THE ONE WOUNDED BY WATER*

I want to go down to the well,
I want to mount Granada's walls
and gaze at the heart transfixed
by the dark drill of the water.

The wounded child moaned
with a crown of hoar-frost.
Ponds, cisterns and fountains
raised their swords to the air.
What a frenzy of love! What a cutting edge!
What night-time murmur! What white death!
What deserts of light were drowning
the sands of dawn!
The child was alone
with the town asleep in his throat.
A fountain spurting from his dreams
assuages the hunger of seaweed.
The child and his anguish, face to face,
were two green entwining rainfalls.
The child stretched out on the earth,
and his anguish writhing.

I want to go down to the well,
I want to die my death in gusts,
I want to fill my heart with moss,
that I may see the one wounded by water.

II *CASIDA DEL LLANTO*

He cerrado mi balcón
porque no quiero oír el llanto
pero por detrás de los grises muros
no se oye otra cosa que el llanto.

Hay muy pocos ángeles que canten,
hay muy pocos perros que ladren,
mil violines caben en la palma de mi mano.
Pero el llanto es un perro inmenso,
el llanto es un ángel inmenso,
el llanto es un violín inmenso,
las lágrimas amordazan al viento
y no se oye otra cosa que el llanto.

II   CASIDA OF THE WEEPING

I have closed up my balcony
because I do not want to hear the weeping;
but from behind the grey walls
nothing is heard but the weeping.

Very few angels can sing,
very few dogs can bark,
a thousand violins fit in the palm of my hand.
But the weeping is an immense dog,
the weeping is an immense angel,
the weeping is an immense violin;
tears muzzle the wind
and nothing is heard but the weeping.

III *CASIDA DE LOS RAMOS*

Por las arboledas del Tamarit
han venido los perros de plomo
a esperar que se caigan los ramos
a esperar que se quiebren ellos solos.

El Tamarit tiene un manzano
con una manzana de sollozos.
Un ruiseñor agrupa los suspiros
y un faisán los ahuyenta por el polvo.

Pero los ramos son alegres,
los ramos son como nosotros:
no piensan en la lluvia y se han dormido
como si fueran árboles, de pronto.

Sentados con el agua en las rodillas
dos valles aguardaban al Otoño.
La penumbra con piso de elefante
empujaba las ramas y los troncos.

Por las arboledas del Tamarit
hay muchos niños de velado rostro
a esperar que se caigan mis ramos
a esperar que se quiebran ellos solos.

III CASIDA OF THE CLUSTERS

Through the groves of the Tamarit
leaden dogs have come
to wait for the clusters to fall,
to wait for them to break on their own.

The Tamarit has an apple-tree
with an apple of sobs.
A nightingale gathers sighs
that a pheasant chases through the dust.

But the clusters are happy,
the clusters are like us.
They are not thinking of rain and have gone to sleep,
suddenly, as if they were trees.

Sitting with the water up to their knees,
two valleys were waiting for autumn.
Dusk with elephantine tread
was pushing the branches and tree-trunks.

Through the groves of the Tamarit
there are many children with veiled face
waiting for my clusters to fall,
waiting for them to break on their own.

IV *CASIDA DE LA MUJER TENDIDA*

Verte desnuda es recordar la Tierra.
La Tierra lisa, limpia de caballos.
La Tierra sin un junco, forma pura
cerrada al porvenir: confín de plata.

Verte es comprender el ansia
de la lluvia que busca débil talle
o la fiebre del mar de inmenso rostro
sin encontrar la luz de su mejilla.

La sangre sonará por las alcobas
y vendrá con espada fulgurante,
pero tú no sabrás dónde se ocultan
el corazón de sapo o la violeta.

Tu vientre es una lucha de raíces,
tus labios son un alba sin contorno,
bajo las rosas tibias de la cama
los muertos gimen esperando turno.

IV CASIDA OF THE RECUMBENT WOMAN

To see you naked is to recall the earth.
The smooth earth, cleared of horses,
the earth reedless, a pure form,
closed to the future: a silver boundary.

To see you naked is to understand
the concern of rain in search of a frail waist,
or the fever of the vast-faced sea
without finding the light of its cheek.

Blood will ring in the alcoves
and appear with lightning swords,
but you'll not know where lie concealed
the heart of toad or the violet.

Your belly is a combat of roots,
your lips a dawn without contour.
Beneath the bed's tepid roses
the dead groan, waiting their turn.

V *CASIDA DEL SUEÑO AL AIRE LIBRE*

Flor de jazmín y toro degollado.
Pavimento infinito. Mapa. Sala. Arpa. Alba.
La niña sueña un toro de jazmines
y el toro es un sangriento crepúsculo que brama.

Si el cielo fuera un niño pequeñito
los jazmines tendrían mitad de noche oscura
y el toro circo azul sin lidiadores
y un corazón al pie de una columna.

Pero el cielo es un elefante
el jazmín es un agua sin sangre
y la niña es un ramo nocturno
por el inmenso pavimento oscuro.

Entre el jazmín y el toro
o garfios de marfil o gente dormida.
En el jazmín un elefante y nubes
y en el toro el esqueleto de la niña.

V CASIDA OF THE OUTDOOR DREAM

Jasmine flower and butchered bull.
Endless pavement. Map. Hall. Harp. Dawn.
The girl imagines a bull of jasmines
and the bull is a gory, bellowing sunset.

If the sky were a tiny boy,
the jasmines would have half a dark night,
and the bull a blue circus without fighters
and a heart at the foot of a column.

But the sky is an elephant
and the jasmine is a bloodless water
and the girl is a nocturnal cluster
along the immense dark pavement.

Between the jasmine and the bull
either ivory hooks or people asleep.
In the jasmine, an elephant and clouds,
and in the bull, the young girl's skeleton.

VI *CASIDA DE LA MANO IMPOSIBLE*

Yo no quiero más que una mano;
una mano herida, si es posible.
Yo no quiero más que una mano
aunque pase mil noches sin lecho.

Sería un pálido lirio de cal.
Sería una paloma amarrada a mi corazón.
Sería el guardián que en la noche de mi tránsito
prohibiera en absoluto la entrada a la luna.

Yo no quiero más que esa mano
para los diarios aceites y la sábana blanca de mi agonía.
Yo no quiero más que esa mano
para tener un ala de mi muerte.

Lo demás todo pasa.
Rubor sin nombre ya. Astro perpetuo.
Lo demás es lo otro; viento triste,
mientras las hojas huyen en bandadas.

VI   *CASIDA OF THE IMPOSSIBLE HAND*

I want no more than a hand,
a wounded hand, if possible.
I want no more than a hand,
though I spend a thousand couchless nights.

It would be a pale lily of lime,
it would be a dove moored to my heart,
it would be the guardian on the night of my passing
to halt, absolutely, the moon's entry.

I want no more than that hand
for the daily ointments and the white shroud of my agony.
I want no more than that hand
to hold a wing of my death.

All other things slip by.
A flash left nameless. A lasting star.
All else is something else; a dismal gust,
as the leaves flee in flocks.

VII *CASIDA DE LA ROSA*

La rosa
no buscaba la aurora:
Casi eterna en su ramo
buscaba otra cosa.

La rosa
no buscaba ni ciencia ni sombra:
Confín de carne y sueño
buscaba otra cosa.

La rosa
no buscaba la rosa:
Inmóvil por el cielo
¡buscaba otra cosa!

VII *CASIDA OF THE ROSE*

The rose
was not looking for dawn:
almost perpetual on its bough,
it was looking for something else.

The rose
was not looking for knowledge or shadow:
boundary of flesh and dream,
it was looking for something else.

The rose,
it was not looking for the rose.
It was looking for something else,
motionless, in the sky.

VIII *CASIDA DE LA MUCHACHA DORADA*

La muchacha dorada
se bañaba en el agua
y el agua se doraba.

Las algas y las ramas
en sombra la asombraban
y el ruiseñor cantaba
por la muchacha blanca.

Vino la noche clara,
turbia de plata mala,
con peladas montañas,
bajo la brisa parda.

La muchacha mojada
era blanca en el agua
y el agua, llamarada.

Vino el alba sin mancha
con cien caras de vaca,
yerta y amortajada
con heladas guirnaldas.

La muchacha de lágrimas,
se bañaba entre llamas
y el ruiseñor lloraba
con las alas quemadas.

VIII   *CASIDA OF THE GOLDEN GIRL*

The golden girl
was bathing in the water
and the water turned gold.

The seaweed and branches
overwhelmed her with shade,
and the nightingale sang
for the girl all white.

Clear night came,
turbid with bad silver,
with bare mountains
under the dusky breeze.

The girl as she dipped
was white in the water
and the water, a blaze.

The immaculate dawn came,
with a thousand bovine faces;
stiff and shrouded
with frozen wreaths.

The girl full of tears
was bathing in the flames,
and the nightingale wept
with its wings burnt.

La muchacha dorada
era una blanca garza
y el agua la doraba.

The golden girl
was a white heron
and the water turned her gold.

IX   *CASIDA DE LAS PALOMAS OSCURAS*

A Claudio Guillén

Por las ramas del laurel
vi dos palomas oscuras:
La una era el sol,
la otra la luna.
Vecinitas; les dije:
¿dónde está mi sepultura?
En mi cola, dijo el sol,
en mi garganta, dijo la luna.
Y yo que estaba caminando
con la tierra por la cintura
vi dos águilas de nieve
y una muchacha desnuda.
La una era la otra
y la muchacha era ninguna.
Aguilitas; les dije:
¿dónde está mi sepultura?
En mi cola, dijo el Sol;
en mi garganta, dijo la Luna.
Por las ramas del laurel
vi dos palomas desnudas.
La una era la otra
y las dos eran ninguna.

IX *CASIDA OF THE DARK DOVES*

TO CLAUDIO GUILLÉN

In the laurel boughs
I saw two dark doves.
One was the sun,
the other the moon.
'Little neighbours,' I said,
'where is my tomb?'
'In my tail,' said the sun.
'In my throat,' said the moon.
And I as I strolled,
the earth to my waist,
saw two snowy eagles
and a naked young girl.
One was the other,
and the young girl was none.
'Little eagles,' I said,
'where is my tomb?'
'In my tail,' said the sun.
'In my throat,' said the moon.
In the laurel boughs
I saw two naked doves.
One was the other
and the two were none.

NOTES

Diván del Tamarit: Tamarit is the Arabic name of a district in Granada in which was situated the *huerta* or orchard-garden of the father of one of Lorca's favourite cousins, Clotilde García Picossi. Lorca had a great affection for this garden and his brother Francisco has suggested that many of the Tamarit poems were written there. *Diván*, sometimes written *Diwan*, is the Arabic word for a collection of short odes or sonnets called *ghazal* (hence the Spanish *gacela*). The most famous *diván* is that of the great Persian lyric poet Hafiz (c. 1325-1389). Hafiz also wrote *kasaid* (hence the Spanish *casida*), idylls or panegyrics. As the distinguished Spanish Arabist Emilio García Gómez points out in the essay appended, Lorca does not employ these terms with any meaningful reference to the Arabic.

Gacela IV

La Vela ('The Watch') is *La Torre de la Vela*, a feature of Granada. Its bell was rung to change the irrigation-water from one channel to another, closing and opening sluice-gates, etc.

Jardín de Cartagena: Borrowed from a popular rhyme:

> *Verbena, verbena,*
> *jardín de Cartagena.*

Gacela XII

Elvira is a corruption of Illiberis, Granada's primitive site whence the Romans moved to neighbouring Garnata (Granada): thus the word frequently crops up in a number of Granadine placenames.

AFTERWORD

by Emilio García Gómez

(The *Nota* of Emilio García Gómez[1] written for a Granadine edition of the *Diván* which was not published.)

In the romantic lounge of the Casa de los Tiros[2], white curtains, clavichord and oil lamp — Federico García Lorca read to us, a group of friends, his new tragedy, *Yerma*. Later, on the spur of the moment, we met to dine in a good eating-place against a background of drunken voices mangling co-plas[3]. Leaning on the table — invisible but present — a young Granadine girl of fifty years ago was listening to the subtly ironic verses which Lorca was reading.

In the conversation, charged with literary electricity, the three a's of Granada sounded frequently. And — speaking, speaking — behind our image of the present city there emerged — as in those figures in geometry in which hidden intersections are pointed out with dotted lines — the idea of another, past Granada, hypothetically purified, where other people were singing in another language to the sound of other guitars.

Exchanging news about literary projects, I was telling Lorca that I intended to devote a book to an Arab magnate — Ibn Zamrak[4] — whose poems had been published in the most luxurious edition the world had ever known: the Alhambra it-self, where they cover the walls, adorn the halls and encircle the fountain-basins of the water jets. Lorca told us then that he had composed, in honour of those ancient Granadine poets, a collection of *casidas* and *gacelas,* that is to say, a *Diván,* which would be called *del Tamarit,* after the name of a family orchard-garden where many of the poems were written.

61

Antonio Gallego Burín[5], as Dean of the Faculty of Letters, asked him for the manuscript. Lorca obliged him with pleasure. Francisco Prieto[6] offered to design the cover. I agreed — I must inform the reader — to write these lines.

In Arabic, *casida* is the name given to every poem of a certain length, with a calculated internal architecture, its detail unimportant, its monorhythmic verse measured according to patterns scrupulously stereotyped. The *gacela* — used chiefly in the Persian lyric — is a short poem, with a preferably erotic subject, adapted to set-rules of technique and containing more than four and less than fifteen verses. *Diván* is a collection of a poet's work, generally catalogued according to the alphabetical order of its rhymes.

I do not think Lorca's use of these names — *diván, gacelas, casidas* — conforms to the above definitions. In this, they are arbitrary. But neither do I think — especially as one is dealing with Lorca — that these poems of his have nothing in common with those oriental names, the literary masks of a romantic carnival, false, empty and distorted.

The poems of the *Diván del Tamarit* are not falsifications or imitations: they are authentically Lorcan. Others will point out their significance in the evolution of the poet's aesthetic, and will perhaps appreciate their increasing force, their concentrated passion and the greater frequency with which, in them, blue veins ingrain and humanise a previously colder marble. Certainly (are there any two things that do not resemble one another in some respect?), it is possible at times to discover in the *Diván* some resemblance to the Arabic lyric. Thus, the presence of the theme of the nocturnal tryst:

La noche no quiere venir,
para que tú no vengas
ni yo pueda ir.

[Night doesn't want to come
  that you may not come
  that I may not go].

or the daring excess of some metaphors:

La penumbra con paso de elefante
empuja las ramas y los troncos.

[Dusk with elephantine tread
  is pushing the branches and tree-trunks].

Again, the verses iridesce with the polychrome of an Iranian
miniature:

Mil caballitos persas se dormían
en la plaza con luna de tu frente.

[A thousand Persian ponies were dozing
  in the moonlit square of your brow].

An accent of love vaguely recalls the morbid pseudo-chastity
of the Bedouin:

Déjame en una ansia de oscuros planetas,
pero no me enseñes tu cintura fresca.

[Leave me to yearn for dark planets
  but do not show me your young waist].

Nevertheless, generally and fortunately, Lorca's poems remain separate from the Arabic verses, to the grammar of which they are not slavishly bound, but rather enslave it; they escape from that pregongorine *gongorismo* in which everything is difficult, but cold and precise, and, instead, scintillate with nebulous intuitions, ineffable sighs, unfulfillable emotions; they are disinterested and there is nothing in them which recalls the elegant mendacity of the dithyramb.

Lorca's love of Granada is a heartfelt coincidence with his ancient countrymen, and, in some way, an imitation of them. No cities are so feminine as Islamic ones, none so loved by poets with such zealous devotion. In these poems, which — like all modern ones — are stripped of proper names, there nonetheless appears, with some frequency, the name of Granada, with a force and grace of the fourth line vocative, such as ancient odes do not have.

Only a Granadine could have felt with such sensitivity that tendency to ruin, that careless and sensual abandonment which — as opposed to fastidious Seville and elegant Córdoba — characterises Granada. Mindful of the city, though not referring to it, those incisive verses speak of

los amarillos que inundan la seda

[the yellows flood the silk].

or of

los arcos rotos en que sufre el tiempo.

[shattered arches where Time mourns].

In the landscape of Granada, set against the prickly lubricity

64

of its fleshy leaves, there has doubtless arisen the daring metaphor:

Pero no ilumines tu limpio desnudo
como un negro cactus abierto en los juncos.

[But do not flare in lucent nakedness
as a black cactus opens out in reeds].

The city itself — white with time and plaster, green with mournful groves — is reflected in those verses in which

Granada era una luna
ahogada entre las yedras.

[Granada was a moon
choking in the ivy].

or in these others, a mirror of exquisite dusks:

Granada era una corza
rosas por las veletas.

[Granada was a hind
roses over the weathervanes].

And only a Granadine could have felt, with such pointed intimacy, the enchantment of Granada's water: rivers, water-jets, channels, fountains, basins, cascades, cisterns, which animate it, dazzle it, drown it, hurl it down slopes and transport it in its current to those desolate horizons in which it eternally dies, drunk with tears, obsessed with an incurable melancholy:

Todas las tardes en Granada,
todas las tardes se muere un niño.
Todas las tardes el agua se sienta
a conversar con sus amigos.

[Every afternoon in Granada,
every afternoon a child dies.
Every afternoon the water sits
to speak with its friends].

The *casidas* entitled 'Of the One Wounded by Water'
and 'Of the Weeping' are a delirious *granadinismo*. . . In the
first, the poet, dynamic, active, possessed of irrespressible
force, enjoys — terrified — the mischievous magic of water:

Quiero bajar al pozo,
quiero morir mi muerte a bocanadas,
quiero llenar mi corazón de musgo
para ver al herido por el agua.

[I want to go down to the well,
I want to die my death in gusts,
I want to fill my heart with moss,
that I may see the one wounded by water].

In the second, on the other hand, he is overcome and yields to
the boundless sadness which the water of Granada inspires. It
is night-time and the balcony has been closed. The angels are
not singing nor are the dogs barking:

Pero el llanto es un perro inmenso,
el llanto es un ángel inmenso,
el llanto es un violín inmenso,

las lágrimas amordazan al viento
y no se oye otra cosa que el llanto.

[But the weeping is an immense dog,
the weeping is an immense angel,
the weeping is an immense violin;
tears muzzle the wind
and nothing is heard but the weeping].

Goethe, as an old man, wrote a *Diván oriental-occidental* which, excepting some strange resemblances, can scarcely be seen as an Islamic lyric. In it, nevertheless, there culminates a tendency to admit great Eastern authors into the ambience of European letters, a movement that started in the 18th century with the presentation of Aladdin in Versailles, and was impeded, stupidly, by a distorted romantic orientalism.

Lorca's *Diván del Tamarit* is neither a joke nor an extravaganza. It is a moving act of homage, written and published* in Granada, where an old Faculty of Letters and an emerging School of Arabic Studies aspire to imbue scientifically in youth the idea that these studies are not just incidental or accidental — a vocation of exoticism or of colonial utilitarianism — but are indispensable to understanding our past and clarifying our tradition.

Would to God science and poetry could achieve their purpose, and on a good day, perhaps still remote, could rescue other Arabists, more fortunate, from this purgatory of the eccentric which now confines them, and enable them to cross over the threshold of other broader humanities.

---

* It was not in fact published as intended. (Tr.)

[1] The eminent Spanish scholar (1905-1995), Head of the School of Arabic Studies in Granada at the time.

[2] Exists still. At the time it housed the local Ministerial Office of Tourism. Gallego Burín (see below) had it restored and endowed with a collection of objects connected with the town's history. The meeting-lounge attracted the literary club or tertulia formed by Lorca, García Gómez, Gallego Burín and others.

[3] Popular Andalusian songs.

[4] Or Ben Zumruk (1333-93), the Arab magnate-poet whose compositions are inscribed all over the Alhambra walls.

[5] 1895-1961.

[6] Francisco Prieto Moreno, a Granadine architect.

The Dedalus Press Poetry Europe Series: